BICYCLE TOURING

BICYCLE TOURING

by Peter B. Mohn

Library of Congress Catalog Card Number: 75-16089
International Standard Book Number: 0-913940-28-3

Reprinted 1978

Crestwood House, Inc., Mankato, Minnesota 56001

Bicyclists ride below the Mount Rushmore National Monument in South Dakota.

PHOTOGRAPHIC CREDITS

Schwinn Bicycle Co., Chicago, Ill.
   3, 8, 13, 14, 15, 18, 22, 23, 25, 26, 28, 29, 31

Wisconsin Department of Natural Resources, Madison, Wis.
   Cover, 7, 11, 12, 17

The Author 6

BICYCLE TOURING

Either the 10-speed lightweight bike or the
smaller 20-inch bike with the "banana" seat is
good for touring.

Almost everyone rides, or can ride a bicycle. Many people these days are riding bicycles for the purpose of seeing new and different things around the country. They are going bicycle touring.

Why ride a bike when we can go by car, bus, train or airplane?

It doesn't cost much. When we provide the energy to pedal, we don't have to worry about gasoline. We spend our money only for the food we eat, the lodging we might need and an occasional bicycle repair.

And any time we feel like stopping to take a closer look at something we can. In bicycle touring we set our own pace. We can do as we please. If something interests us, we can learn more about it.

This trail — for bicycles only — stretches more than 60 miles across the state of Wisconsin.

More and more people in North America are touring on bicycles these days. Europeans have done it for many years.

Bicycle touring is a healthy, friendly way of going places. It is good exercise. And we can meet some very nice people in the process.

We can take a bicycle tour for a few hours or a whole day. Or, if we have lots of time, we can take a tour that covers hundreds of miles and lasts several days. Some people spend whole summers touring on their bikes.

For the one-day bicycle tourist, many cities have set up bikeways on streets or parkways. Some times, they will block off the streets for bikes only.

In some states, long stretches of bike trails have been set aside for the people who want to ride longer distances, and programmed tours are available. The biker can ride for mile after mile and never have to worry about automobile traffic.

Touring in groups can be fun. The cyclists not only can be together, they can help one another in an emergency.

Many people ride bicycles for some useful purpose. They go to school, to the store or to work. But just like in Europe, we are learning that the bike is as good on vacation as it is during the workaday week.

So the numbers of bicycles in the country have grown, and it's not just the fancy ten-speeds. People who want to can tour almost as easily on a plain, single speed bicycle with a coaster brake. Or two people can tour on a tandem bicycle.

To take a bike tour, we should start with a plan. Many tours are planned during periods of bad weather, when biking would be difficult or even impossible. Planning for a ride in good weather often is a good way of being able to forget the bad weather.

One way of keeping up with the adults is to ride a two-seat or tandem bicycle, like the one on the right.

The very young bike tourer can be backpacked
or can ride in a special seat over the rear
wheel.

Planning a bike trip is like trying to see ourselves taking it. Good road maps and other guides to the area we're going to ride through are needed to make the plan.

With the maps in front of us and the other guides, telling where parks, stopover points and interesting areas are, we can judge the distances we will ride and the things we will see each day.

Some say that planning a bike tour is almost as much fun as taking it.

At sundown, bike tourists should stop for the night.

In riding through California, we might pass the
Golden Gate Bridge.

Bicycling by the Gateway Arch in St. Louis, Missouri.

The trip plan is good for two reasons. It helps us set a pace for the tour, and it gives others a record of where we're going to be in case they need to get in touch with us.

The plan also helps us know when we're going to be pedaling hard across country and when we'll be stopping to spend some time sightseeing, fishing or just goofing off. Since there's a lot of that in almost every bicycle tour, time should be allowed for it.

If we are on an organized tour, much of this will be done for us by the organizers. They will make arrangements for overnight stays in campgrounds and perhaps even provide a "sag wagon" for the bicycle or rider who just can't make it at one time or other.

After the plan, there are two more things we need.

The first is that our bicycle must be in good condition. If we begin a trip with a bike that is not working well, we're asking for trouble along the way. Everything — tires, wheels, chain, pedals and steering parts — should work well.

15

To get the bicycle into good condition, we should check it carefully. Is there good tread on the tires and are they properly inflated?

Do the brakes work well? Do the wheels spin evenly and without resistance? Are the pedals on tight? Are the handlebars on tight and at the proper height? Is the saddle (or seat) at the proper height?

The second is that we must be in good condition. A bicycle tour will be no fun if we can't finish it. So if we're not used to riding a mile or two — or **25** miles — we should get ourselves into condition for the tour. Being in good condition is good for our health.

Getting ourselves into condition for a tour can be a simple matter. Almost any active thing we do will help. Walking, jogging or running will give us a greater amount of endurance for a bicycle tour. If the weather is good, we might even take our bikes on longer and longer rides.

Very often, the people who tour on their bikes in good weather also hike or go canoeing or participate in some other back-to-nature sport. Doing one thing helps people to stay in shape for other sports.

These things can be done during non-biking weather. Like planning the trip, they can be done while thinking about the fun we're going to have on the tour.

With a good bike and a smooth pathway, we
can travel many miles in a day's time.

Some parkways are reserved for people, bikes
and horses only.

Many bicyclists have a very basic understanding of how their bikes work. This is very useful, since they can make minor repairs to their bikes while touring.

We should know, for example, how to fix a flat tire. Or how to adjust the caliper brakes on a three, five or ten-speed bike if we're riding one. Being able to do these things means that if something goes wrong on a trip, it won't force us to quit.

What about the speed bikes?

Most of us started riding on single-speed bikes with coaster brakes. When we pedaled hard, we moved. When we back-pedaled, the coaster brake in the rear hub caused us to stop.

Experienced bikers say the ten-speed bike is the best for touring. Having the ten speeds helps with hill climbing or getting the best performance on level land.

This does not mean that we cannot tour on a single speed bicycle, however. Whatever we can pedal can take us where we want to go.

PROPER BICYCLE FIT AND ADJUSTMENT

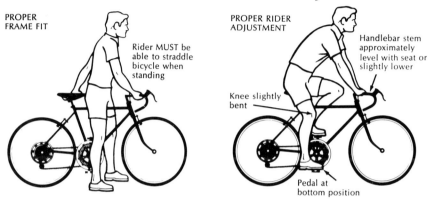

PROPER
FRAME FIT

Rider MUST be able to straddle bicycle when standing

PROPER RIDER
ADJUSTMENT

Handlebar stem approximately level with seat or slightly lower

Knee slightly bent

Pedal at bottom position

The second, or middle, gear of a three-speed bicycle is probably just like the normal gear of a single speed bike. That means that we have one lower gear — for hills — and one higher gear — for speed — than a single speed bike.

The third, or middle, gear on a five-speed bicycle is probably just about like a single-speed. The higher gears in the five-speed cluster, which is mounted on the rear wheel, are for speed and the lower ones for power. On a ten-speed bicycle, there are five gears on the rear wheel and two on the chainwheel by the pedals. The person who rides a ten-speed bike has 10 different gear combinations.

The more complicated the bike, the more we must pay attention to its maintenance. Every moving part must be kept clean and well-lubricated. After every ride, we must take a little time to clean and oil our bike.

What do we take on a tour?

That depends on how long it is and what we plan to do. A day's trip might require only a sandwich or two and something to drink. A week's trip might require all the things for camping like a tent, a sleeping bag, cooking utensils and a change or two of clothing.

Like most back-to-nature sports, bicycling is a travel-light sport. We should carry as little as possible and plan on finding or buying various supplies we need along the way.

We should never overlook the idea of finding food along the way. We might see a wild berry patch by the side of the road. Or we might take a hook and line and hope that we might be able to catch a fish.

Other things we should take include a poncho or some kind of rain suit, a small tool kit with wrenches and levers for changing tires, insect repellent and perhaps even a cream or lotion which helps prevent sunburn.

21

We should always pack the heavy things low. This will help keep the bicycle in better balance. There are pannier bags which fit like saddlebags over front or rear wheels, handlebar bags and bags which attach to the seat of the bike. Many of the handlebar bags have pockets of clear plastic for waterproof map storage.

If we take a supply of water, we can put it in a frame-mounted bottle. We can also attach a slender, lightweight tire pump to the bicycle frame.

On a short, day-long tour, we probably wouldn't need all these things, but they are very handy for overnight trips.

With baskets on the bicycle, it becomes handy for going to the store, delivering papers or carrying books.

In many places it is possible to rent tandem
bikes for an hour — or a day — of
sightseeing and exercise.

Before the ride begins, we should check the
weather. This not only tells us whether we should ride,
but it may give us a clue as to how to dress for it. Unless
we absolutely have to ride, biking in rainy weather is
no fun. And if we're going to have the wind in our
faces all day, that will slow us down.

If the wind is at our backs, however, we might
be able to plan on reaching our destination more
quickly.

Bikers who tour in groups on trails or on roads
usually ride in single file, or in a staggered formation.
The lead rider creates a pocket of air for the followers
to pedal in and it makes it easier for them. Various

members of the group will trade off in the lead because that's harder work.

Most states require bicyclists to ride single file on the right side of the road. We should remember to wear relatively bright clothing so the drivers of cars can see us.

And before we leave, we should make sure that someone knows what our trip plans are. This will make it easier for them to find us in an emergency. If we're taking a long trip, we should remember to send postcards home to let them know we're okay.

Once we're off on our trip, we're on our own. If both we and our bikes are in good condition, it should be fun.

We'll probably start by pedaling through areas we know well, but as we get farther from home, we're likely to see all kinds of new and interesting things.

There are many bicycle clubs in the country.
Some have their own distinctive riding
uniforms.

When riding on designated bike paths, we may not have to follow the single file rule. But we should be ready to move to the right side to make way for oncoming bikes.

With our trip plan always in mind, we can stop to look at things or do something along the way.

In riding the public roads, we must observe the laws of the state or city. Bicycle laws are quite different from state to state and city to city. We should know them all.

Most states require bicyclists to signal their turns. Signals are made with the left hand and arm. If the arm is stretched out straight and to the left, it means we are turning left. If we bend the arm at the elbow and hold our left hand up, we're turning right.

Riding through the city, we should be very careful of parked cars. Many bikers have been rudely dumped from their bikes and injured because a car door opened suddenly in front of them.

We must use our eyes to find out what's in front of us and our ears to tell what's behind. Even in a strong wind, we can hear the noise of a car behind us, and it's up to us to move as far to the right of the road as possible.

We should try to set a consistent pace and maintain about the same number of pedal strokes each minute. If our bicycles have more than one gear, we should maintain that pace in the gear that's most comfortable.

Most experienced bicycle tourers keep their hands well down on the handlebars of their European style

Plenty of sun and plenty of scenery await the
bicycle tourist.

bicycles. That way, their hands are close to the brakes,
more convenient to the shifters, and the wind resistance
is less with the body low.

As the scenery changes in front of us, we can be
happy that we are seeing the change and proud that
we're doing it under our own power.

A springtime bicycle tour might take us past all
kinds of flowering fruit trees. The same tour in the
fall might show the hardwood trees ablaze with color
shortly before the leaves drop.

In spring, summer and fall, all our senses may be
enriched. The sounds of birds or farm animals, the
sight of growing crops and the smell of newly-mown
hay may be just a few of the things we will experience.

In an area of historic interests, we can stop and
read roadside markers which will tell us what hap-
pened there in the past, or we might just settle into a
shady wayside, have lunch and take a short nap.

A rest stop can be made anywhere, but it's often
better to stop at a park or wayside where there will be
water, toilets and maybe even picnic tables.

27

The bicycle with the 20-inch wheel will usually be our first.
As we grow and our legs get longer, we can move on to
a bike with 26 or 27 inch wheels.

As the day goes on, we might stop a little more frequently to get out of the hot sun, and each biker in the group should watch the others for signs of sunburn.

Bike touring is fun, but there are a few things which can make it difficult.

The first is the weather. Very often in the summer, lines of thunderstorms will pass over the country and they can leave us soaking wet and sometimes frightened. If a thunderstorm comes along, we should seek shelter in a building of some kind.

The next is the dog. The dog may be man's best friend, but some of them are a biker's worst enemy. Some dogs will not only chase, they will bite bicyclists. Every biker has his own ideas about what to do with dogs. There are sprays, loud horns and other things to chase them off.

Some even try to pedal harder and outrun the dog, but few succeed, unless the dog is small. Some dogs become more timid when the person on two wheels dismounts and faces the dog on two feet.

Another problem we face when riding is ourselves. Riding will seem to be so easy that we get careless. When we aren't paying attention, we can be hurt. We must keep our bikes and ourselves under control at all times.

It's fun to ride fast, but there's a point at which our bikes can be ridden no faster. We should never ride so fast that we cannot come to a smooth stop under all conditions.

The palm trees and light clothing mean these bicyclists are touring in the South.

Planning our bicycle tour is fun. So is preparing for it. We often think that taking it is the most fun of all.

Like any back to nature sport, bike touring is something we do ourselves, and the feeling of having done it — once we are finished — is probably the best of all.

We can look back on the one mile, the ten miles or the thousand miles we have ridden. We can remember the things we have seen, the roads or trails we have ridden and the people we have met.

Chances are very good that if we planned and prepared well for the trip we took, we will have enjoyed it and we can tell our friends about it and make them envious.

Who knows?

The next tour we take, they might join us!

When this bicycle tour is over, the tourists are
very likely to start planning their next trip
right away.